ANTIGONE

by SOPHOCLES

Perfection Learning Corporation
Logan, Iowa

Cover Art Copyright 1987. Perfection Learning Corporation,
Logan, Iowa   Printed in U.S.A.

26 27 28 29 30 PP 08

Persons Represented

Antigone, daughter of Oedipus, late king of Thebes.

Ismene, daughter of Oedipus, late king of Thebes.

Creon, brother to Jocasta, late queen of Thebes, Captain-general of the army, and successor to the throne.

A Sentinel.

Haemon, son to Creon, betrothed to Antigone.

Tiresias, a seer.

A Messenger in attendance on Creon.

Eurydice, wife to Creon.

The Chorus is composed of Senators of Thebes.

Guards; Attendants; a Boy leading Tiresias.

ANTIGONE

Scene, before the Royal Palace at Thebes.
Time, early morning. Enter ANTIGONE
and ISMENE.

Antigone. Ismene, dear in very sisterhood,
Do you perceive how Heaven upon us two
Means to fulfil, before we come to die,
Out of all ills that grow from Oedipus—
What not, indeed? for there's no sorrow or
harm,
No circumstance of scandal or of shame
I have not seen, among your griefs, and
mine.
And now again, what is this word they
say
Our Captain-general proclaimed but now
To the whole city? Did you hear and heed?
Or are you blind, while pains of enemies
Are passing on your friends?
Ismene.   Antigone,
To me no tidings about friends are come,

1

Pleasant or grievous, ever since we two
Of our two brothers were bereft, who died
Both in one day, each by the other's hand.
And since the Argive host in this same
  night
Took itself hence, I have heard nothing
  else,
To make me happier, or more miserable.
Antigone. I knew as much; and for that
  reason made you
Go out of doors — to tell you privately.
Ismene. What is it? I see you have some
  mystery.
Antigone. What! has not Creon to the tomb
  preferred
One of our brothers, and with contumely
Withheld it from the other? Eteocles
Duly, they say, even as by law was due,
He hid beneath the earth, rendering him
  honour
Among the dead below; but the dead body
Of Polynices, miserably slain,
They say it has been given out publicly
None may bewail, none bury, all must
  leave
Unwept, unsepulchred, a dainty prize
For fowl that watch, gloating upon their
  prey!
This is the matter he has had pro-
  claimed—

2

Excellent Creon! for your heed, they say,
And mine, I tell you — mine! and he
    moves hither,
Meaning to announce it plainly in the ears
Of such as do not know it, and to declare
It is no matter of small moment; he
Who does any of these things shall surely
    die;
The citizens shall stone him in the streets.
So stands the case. Now you will quickly
    show
If you are worthy of your birth or no.
Ismene. But O rash heart, what good, if it be
    thus,
Could I effect, helping or hindering?
Antigone. Look, will you join me? will you
    work with me?
Ismene. In what attempt? What mean you?
Antigone.   Help me lift
The body up—
Ismene.   What, would you bury him?
Against the proclamation?
Antigone.   My own brother
And yours I will! If you will not, I will;
I shall not prove disloyal.
Ismene.   You are mad!
When Creon has forbidden it?
Antigone.   From mine own
He has no right to stay me.
Ismene.   Alas, O sister,

Think how our father perished! self-
   convict—
Abhorred — dishonoured — blind — his
   eyes put out
By his own hand! How she who was at
   once
His wife and mother with a knotted noose
Laid violent hands on her own life! And
   how
Our two unhappy brothers in one day
Each on his own head by the other's hand
Wrought common ruin! We now left
   alone—
Do but consider how most miserably
We too shall perish, if despite of law
We traverse the behest or power of kings.
We must remember we are women born,
Unapt to cope with men; and, being ruled
By mightier than ourselves, we have to
   hear
These things — and worse. For my part,
   I will ask
Pardon of those beneath, for what
   perforce
I needs must do, but yield obedience
To them that walk in power; to exceed
Is madness, and not wisdom.

Antigone.   Then in future
   I will not bid you help me; nor henceforth,

4

Though you desire, shall you, with my
    good will,
Share what I do. Be what seems right to
    you;
Him will I bury. Death, so met, were
    honour;
And for that capital crime of piety,
Loving and loved, I will lie by his side.
Far longer is there need I satisfy
Those nether Powers, than powers on
    earth; for there
For ever must I lie. You, if you will,
Hold up to scorn what is approved of
    Heaven!
Ismene. I am not one to cover things with
    scorn;
But I was born too feeble to contend
Against the state.
Antigone. Yes, you can put that forward;
    But I will go and heap a burial mound
    Over my most dear brother.
Ismene.   My poor sister,
How beyond measure do I fear for you!
Antigone. Do not spend fear on me. Shape
    your own course.
Ismene. At least announce it, then, to
    nobody,
But keep it close, as I will.
Antigone.   Tell it, tell it!

You'll cross me worse, by far, if you keep
  silence—
Not publish it to all.

Ismene.   Your heart beats hotly
For chilling work!

Antigone.   I know that those approve
Whom I most need to please.

Ismene.   If you could do it!
But you desire impossibilities.

Antigone. Well, when I find I have no power
  to stir,
I will cease trying.

Ismene.   But things impossible
'Tis wrong to attempt at all.

Antigone.   If you will say it,
I shall detest you soon; and you will justly
Incur the dead man's hatred. Suffer me
And my unwisdom to endure the weight
Of what is threatened. I shall meet with
  nothing
More grievous, at the worst, than death,
  with honour.

Ismene. Then go, if you will have it: and
  take this with you,
You go on a fool's errand!

                [Exit ANTIGONE.

                      Lover true
To your beloved, none the less, are you!
[Exit.

Enter THEBAN SENATORS, as Chorus.

Chorus.
I. 1.

Sunbeam bright! Thou fairest ray
  That ever dawned on Theban eyes
    Over the portals seven!
O orb of aureate day,
  How glorious didst thou rise
    O'er Dirca's streams, shining from heaven,
Him, the man with shield of white
Who came from Argos in armour dight
Hurrying runagate o'er the plain,
Jerking harder his bridle rein;
Who by Polynices' quarrellous broil
Stirred up in arms to invade our soil
    With strident cries as an eagle flies
  Swooped down on the fields before him,
'Neath cover of eagle pinion white
As drifted snow, a buckler bright
    On many a breast, and a horsetail crest
  From each helm floating o'er him.
I. 2.

Yawning with many a blood-stained spear
  Around our seven-gated town
    High o'er the roofs he stood;
Then, or ever a torch could sear

With flames the rampart-crown—
   Or ever his jaws were filled with
    blood
Of us and ours, lo, he was fled!
Such clatter of war behind him spread,
Stress too sore for his utmost might
Matched with the Dragon in the fight;
For Zeus abhors tongue-glorious boasts;
And straightway as he beheld their hosts,
Where on they rolled, covered with gold,
   Streaming in mighty eddy,
Scornfully with a missile flame
He struck down Capaneus, as he came
Uplifting high his victory-cry
   At the topmost goal already.

II. 1.

Tantalus-like aloft he hung, then fell;
   Earth at his fall resounded;
Even as, maddened by the Bacchic spell,
   On with torch in hand he bounded,
    Breathing blasts of hate.
So the stroke was turned aside,
   Mighty Ares rudely dealing
Others elsewhere, far and wide,
   Like a right-hand courser wheeling
    Round the goals of fate.
For captains seven at portals seven
Found each his match in the combat even,

And left on the field both sword and
    shield
    As a trophy to Zeus, who o'erthrew
      them;
Save the wretched twain, who against
      each other
Though born of one father, and one
    mother,
Laid lances at aim — to their own death
    c a m e ,
    And the common fate that slew them.

II. 2.

But now loud Victory returns at last
    On Theban chariots smiling
Let us begin oblivion of the past,
    Memories of late war beguiling
      Into slumber sound.
  Seek we every holy shrine;
    There begin the night-long chorus;
  Let the Theban Boy divine,
    Bacchus, lead the way before us,
    Shaking all the ground.
Leave we the song: the King is here;
Creon, Menoeceus' son, draws near;
To the function strange — like the heaven-
    sent change
  Which has raised him newly to power:
What counsel urging — what ends of
    state,

That he summons us to deliberate,
The elders all, by his herald's call,
   At a strange unwonted hour?
    Enter CREON, attended.
Creon. Sirs, for the ship of state — the Gods
   once more,
After much rocking on a stormy surge,
Set her on even keel. Now therefore you,
You of all others, by my summoners
I bade come hither; having found you first
Right loyal ever to the kingly power
In Laius' time; and next, while Oedipus
Ordered the commonwealth; and since his
   fall,
With steadfast purposes abiding still,
Circling their progeny. Now, since they
   perished,
Both on one day, slain by a two-edged
   fate,
Striking and stricken, sullied with a stain
Of mutual fratricide, I, as you know,
In right of kinship nearest to the dead,
Possess the throne and take the supreme
   power.
Howbeit it is impossible to know
The spirit of any man, purpose or will,
Before it be displayed by exercise
In government and laws. To me, I say,
Now as of old, that pilot of the state
Who set no hand to the best policy,

But remains tongue-tied through some
    terror, seems
Vilest of men. Him too, who sets a friend
Before his native land, I prize at nothing.
God, who seest all things always, witness
    it!
If I perceive, where safety should have
    been,
Mischief advancing toward my citizens,
I will not sit in silence; nor account
As friend to me the country's enemy;
But thus I deem: she is our ark of safety;
And friends are made then only, when,
    embarked
Upon her deck, we ride the seas upright.
Such are the laws by which I mean to
    further
This city's welfare; and akin to these
I have given orders to the citizens
Touching the sons of Oedipus. Eteocles,
Who in this city's quarrel fought and fell,
The foremost of our champions in the
    fray,
They should entomb with the full sanctity
Of rites that solemnize the downward
    road
Of their dead greatest. Him the while, his
    brother,
That Polynices who, returning home

A banished man, sought to lay waste with
    fire
His household Gods, his native country —
    sought
To glut himself with his own kindred's
    blood,
Or carry them away to slavery,
It has been promulgated to the city
No man shall bury, none should wail for
    him;
Unsepulchred, shamed in the eyes of men,
His body shall be left to be devoured
By dogs and fowls of the air. Such is my
    will.
Never with me shall wicked men usurp
The honours of the righteous; but whoe'er
Is friendly to this city shall, by me,
Living or dead, be honoured equally.

I Senator. Creon Menoeceus' son, we hear
    your pleasure
Both on this city's friend, and on her foe;
It is your sovereignty's prerogative
To pass with absolute freedom on the
    dead,
And us, who have survived them.

Creon.   Please to see
What has been said performed.

I Senator.   That charge confer
On some one who is younger.

Creon.   Of the body?

Sentries are set, already.

I Senator.   Then what else
   Is there, besides, which you would lay on
   us?

Creon. Not to connive at disobedience.

I Senator. There's no such fool as to
   embrace his death.

Creon. Death is the penalty. But men right
   often
   Are brought to ruin, through their dreams
   of gain.

                    Enter a Sentinel.

Sentinel. My lord, I will not say —
   "breathless with speed
   I come, plying a nimble foot;" for truly
   I had a many sticking-points of thought,
   Wheeling about to march upon my rear.
   For my heart whispered me all sorts of
   counsel;
   "Poor wretch, why go, to meet thy
   sentence?" — "Wretch,
   Tarrying again? If Creon hear the news
   From others' lips, how shalt thou then not
   rue it?"
   Out of this whirligig it came to pass
   I hastened — at my leisure; a short road,
   Thus, becomes long. Nevertheless at last
   It won the day to come hither, to your
   presence;

And speak I will, though nothing have to
    say;
For I come clinging to the hope that I
Can suffer nothing — save my destiny.
Creon. Well — and what caused you this
    disheartenment?
Sentinel. First let me tell you what concerns
    myself.
I do protest, I neither did the deed,
Nor saw it done, whoever 'twas who did it;
Nor should I rightly come to any harm.
Creon. At all events you are a good
    tactician,
And fence the matter off all round. But
    clearly
You have some strange thing to tell?
Sentinel.   Yes. Serious tidings
Induce much hesitation.
Creon.   Once for all
Please to speak out, and make an end, and
    g o .
Sentinel. Why, I am telling you. That body
    some one
Has just now buried — sprinkled thirsty
    dust
Over the form — added the proper rites,
And has gone off.
Creon.   What say you? What man dared
To do it?

14

Sentinel.   I know not. There was no dint there
Of any mattock, not a sod was turned;
Merely hard ground and bare, without a break,
Without a rut from wheels; it was some workman
Who left no mark. When the first day-sentry
Shewed what had happened, we were all dismayed.
The body had vanished; not indeed interred,
But a light dust lay on it, as if poured out
By one who shunned the curse; and there appeared
No trace that a wild beast, or any hound,
Had come, or torn the carcase. Angry words
Were bandied up and down, guard blaming guard,
And blows had like to end it, none being by
To hinder; for each one of us in turn
Stood culprit, none convicted, but the plea
"I know not" passed. Ready were we to take
Hot iron in hand, or pass through fire, and call

The Gods to witness, that we neither did
　　it,
　Nor were accessory to any man
Who compassed it, or did it. So at last,
When all our searching proved to be in
　　vain,
There speaks up one, who made us, every
　　man,
Hang down our heads for fear, knowing
　　no way
To say him nay, or without scathe
　　comply,
His burden was, this business must be
　　carried
To you, without reserve. That voice
　　prevailed;
And me, poor wretch, the lot condemns to
　　get
This piece of luck. I come a post unwilling,
I well believe it, to unwilling ears;
None love the messenger who brings bad
　　news.
I Senator. My lord, my heart misgave me
　　from the first
　This must be something more than
　　natural.
Creon. Truce to your speech, before I choke
　　with rage,
　Lest you be found at once grey-beard and
　　fool!

To say that guardian deities would care
For this dead body, is intolerable.
Could they, by way of supereminent
   honour
Paid to a benefactor, give him burial,
Who came to fire their land, their pillared
   fanes
And sacred treasures, and set laws at
   nought?
Or do you see Gods honouring the bad?
'Tis false. These orders from the first
   some people
Hardly accepted, murmuring at me,
Shaking their heads in secret, stiffening
Uneasy necks against this yoke of mine.
They have suborned these sentinels to do
   it,
I know that well. No such ill currency
Ever appeared, as money to mankind:
This is it that sacks cities, this routs out
Men from their homes, and trains and
   turns astray
The minds of honest mortals, setting
   them
Upon base actions; this made plain to men
Habits of all misdoing, and cognizance
Of every work of wickedness. Howbeit
Such hireling perpetrators, in the end,
Have wrought so far, that they shall pay
   for it.

So surely as I live to worship Jove,
Know this for truth; I swear it in your
  ears;
Except you find and bring before my face
The real actor in this funeral,
Death, by itself, shall not suffice for you,
Before, hung up alive, you have revealed
The secret of this outrage; that henceforth
You may seek plunder — not without
  respect
Of where your profit lies; and may be
  taught
It is not good to covet all men's pay;
For mark you! by corruption few men
  thrive,
And many come to mischief.
Sentinel.   Have I leave
  To say a word, or shall I turn and go?
Creon. Cannot you see your prating tortures
  me?
Sentinel. Pricks you how deep? In the ears,
  or to the spleen?
Creon. Why do you gauge my chafing,
  where it lies?
Sentinel. Your heart-ache were the doer's,
  your ear-ache mine.
Creon. Out, what a bare-faced babbler born
  art thou!
Sentinel. Never the actor in this business,
  though!

Creon. Yes, and for money you would sell
    your soul!

Sentinel. Plague on it! 'tis hard, a man
    should be suspicious,

And with a false suspicion!

Creon.   Yes, suspicion;

  Mince it as best you may. Make me to
    know

  Whose are these doings, or you shall soon
    allow

  Left-handed gains work their own
    punishment.

                              [Exit.

Sentinel. I wish he may be found. Chance
    must decide.

  Whether or no, you will not, certainly,

  See me returning hither. Heaven be
praised

  I am in safety, past all thought or dream!

                              [Exit.

Chorus
I. 1.

Much is there passing strange;
  Nothing surpassing mankind.
He it is loves to range
Over the ocean hoar,
Thorough the surges' roar,
  South winds raging behind;
Earth, too, wears he away,
  The Mother of Gods on high,

Tireless, free from decay;
With team he furrows the ground,
And the ploughs go round and round,
　　As year on year goes by.

I. 2.

The bird-tribes, light of mind,
　　The races of beasts of prey,
And sea-fish after their kind,
Man, abounding in wiles,
Entangles in his toils
　　And carries captive away.
The roamers over the hill,
　　The field-inhabiting deer,
By craft he conquers, at will;
He bends beneath his yoke
The neck of the steed unbroke,
　　And pride of the upland steer.

II. 1.

He has gotten him speech, and fancy
　　breeze-betost,
　　And for the state instinct of order meet;
He has found him shelter from the chilling
　　frost
　　Of a clear sky, and from the arrowy
　　sleet;
Illimitable in cunning, cunning-less
　　He meets no change of fortune that can
　　come;
He has found escape from pain and
　　helplessness;

Only he knows no refuge from the tomb.
II. 2.
Now bends he to the good, now to the ill,
  With craft of art, subtle past reach of
    sight;
Wresting his country's laws to his own
    will,
  Spurning the sanctions of celestial
    right;
High in the city, he is made city-less,
  Whoso is corrupt, for his impiety;
He that will work the works of wicked-
    ness,
  Let him not house, let him not hold,
    with me!
  At this monstrous vision I stand in
  Doubt! How dare I say, well knowing
    her
  That this maid is not — Antigone!
    Daughter of Oedipus!
  Hapless child, of a hapless father!
  Sure — ah surely they did not find thee
  Madly defying our king's command-
    ments,
    And so prisoner bring thee here?
Enter Sentinel with ANTIGONE.
Sentinel. This is the woman who has done
    the deed.
  We took her burying him. Where's Creon?
I Senator.   Here

Comes he again, out of the house, at need.

Enter   CREON.

Creon. What is it? In what fit season come I
forth?

Sentinel. My lord, I see a man should never
vow
   He will not do a thing, for second
   thoughts
   Bely the purpose. Truly I could have
   sworn
   It would be long indeed ere I came hither
   Under that hail of threats you rained on
   me.
   But since an unforeseen happy surprise
   Passes all other pleasing out of measure,
   I come, though I forswore it mightily,
   Bringing this maiden, who was caught in
   act
   To set that bier in order. Here, my lord,
   No lot was cast; this windfall is to me,
   And to no other. Take her, now, yourself;
   Examine and convict her, as you please;
   I wash my hands of it, and ought, of right,
   To be clean quit of the scrape, for good
   and all.

Creon. You seized — and bring — her! In
what way, and whence?

Sentinel. Burying that man, herself! You
know the whole.

Creon. Are you in earnest? Do you
    understand
What you are saying?
Sentinel.   Yes, that I saw this girl
    Burying that body you forbade to bury.
    Do I speak clear and plain?
Creon.   How might this be,
    That she was seen, and taken in the act?
Sentinel. Why thus it happened. When we
    reached the place,
    Wrought on by those dread menacings
      from you,
    We swept away all dust that covered up
    The body, and laid the clammy limbs
      quite bare,
    And windward from the summit of the
      hill,
    Out of the tainted air that spread from
      him,
    We sat us down, each, as it might be,
      rousing
    His neighbour with a clamour of abuse,
    Wakening him up, whenever any one
    Seemed to be slack in watching. This went
      on,
    Till in mid air the luminous orb of day
    Stood, and the heat grew sultry. Suddenly
    A violent eddy lifted from the ground
    A hurricane, a trouble of the sky;
    Ruffling all foliage of the woodland plain

It filled the horizon; the vast atmosphere
Thickened to meet it; we, closing our eyes,
Endured the Heaven-sent plague. After a
    while,
When it had ceased, there stands this
    maiden in sight,
And wails aloud, shrill as the bitter note
Of the sad bird, when as she finds the
    couch
Of her void nest robbed of her young; so
    she,
Soon as she sees the body stripped and
    bare,
Bursts out in shrieks, and calls down
    curses dire
On their heads who had done it.
    Straightway then
She gathers handfuls of dry dust, and
    brings them,
And from a shapely brazen cruse held
    high
She crowns the body with drink-offerings,
Once, twice, and thrice. We at the sight
    rushed forward,
And trapped her, nothing daunted, on the
    spot;
And taxed her with the past offence, and
    this
The present. Not one whit did she deny;
A pleasant though a pitiful sight to me;

For nothing's sweeter than to have got off
In person; but to bring into mischance
Our friends is pitiful. And yet to pay
No more than this is cheap, to save one's
    life.

Creon. Do you, I say — you, with your
    downcast brow—
    Own or deny that you have done this
    deed?

Antigone. I say I did it; I deny it not.

Creon. Take yourself hence, whither you
    will, sir knave;
    You are acquitted of a heavy charge.

                  [Exit Sentinel.

    Now tell me, not at length, but in brief
    space,
    Knew you the order not to do it?

Antigone.   Yes,
    I knew it; what should hinder? It was
    plain.

Creon. And you made free to overstep my
    law?

Antigone. Because it was not Zeus who
    ordered it,
    Nor Justice, dweller with the Nether
    Gods,
    Gave such a law to men; nor did I deem
    Your ordinance of so much binding force,
    As that a mortal man could overbear

The unchangeable unwritten code of
Heaven;
This is not of today and yesterday,
But lives for ever, having origin
Whence no man knows: whose sanctions I
were loath
In Heaven's sight to provoke, fearing the
will
Of any man. I knew that I should die—
How otherwise? even although your voice
Had never so prescribed. And that I die
Before my hour is due, that I count gain.
For one who lives in many ills, as I—
How should he fail to gain by dying? Thus
To me the pain is light, to meet this fate;
But had I borne to leave the body of him
My mother bare unburied, then, indeed,
I might feel pain; but as it is, I cannot,
And if my present action seems to you
Foolish — 'tis like I am found guilty of
folly
At a fool's mouth!

I Senator.　　　　Lo you, the spirit stout
Of her stout father's child — unapt to
bend
Beneath misfortune!

Creon.　　　　　　But be well assured,
Tempers too stubborn are the first to fail;
The hardest iron from the furnace, forged
To stiffness, you may see most frequently

Shivered and broken; and the chafing
    steeds
I have known governed with a slender
    curb.
It is unseemly that a household drudge
Should be misproud; but she was
    conversant
With outrage, ever since she passed the
    bounds
Laid down by law; then hard upon that
    deed
Comes this, the second outrage, to exult
And triumph in her deed. Truly if here
She wield such powers uncensured, she is
    man,
I woman! Be she of my sister born,
Or nearer to myself than the whole band
Of our domestic tutelary Jove,
She, and the sister — for her equally
I charge with compassing this funeral—
Shall not escape a most tremendous
    doom.
And call her; for within the house but now
I saw her, frenzied and beside herself;
And it is common for the moody sprite
Of plotters in the dark to no good end
To have been caught, planning its
    knavery,
Before the deed is acted. None the less
I hate it, when one taken in misdoing

Straight seeks to gloss the facts!

Antigone.   Would you aught more
Than take my life, whom you did catch?

Creon.   Not I;
Take that, take all.

Antigone.   Then why do you delay?
Since naught is pleasing of your words to
  me,
Or, as I trust, can ever please, so mine
Must needs be unacceptable to you.
And yet from whence could I have
  gathered praise
More worthily, than from depositing
My own brother in a tomb? These, all of
  them,
Would utter one approval, did not fear
Seal up their lips. 'Tis tyranny's privilege,
And not the least — power to declare and
  do
What it is minded.

Creon.   You, of all this people,
Are singular in your discernment.

Antigone.   Nay,
They too discern; they but refrain their
  tongues
At your behest.

Creon.   And you are not ashamed
That you deem otherwise?

Antigone.   It is no shame
To pay respect to our own flesh and blood.

Creon. And his dead foeman, was not he your brother
As well?

Antigone. Yes, the same sire's and mother's son.

Creon. Why pay, then, honours which are wrongs to him?

Antigone. The dead clay makes no protest.

Creon. Not although
His with a villain's share your reverence?

Antigone. It was no bondman perished, but a brother.

Creon. Spoiling, I say, this country; while his rival
Stood for it.

Antigone. All the same, these rites are due
To the underworld.

Creon. But not in equal measure
Both for the good man and the bad.

Antigone. Who knows
This is not piety there?

Creon. The enemy
Can never be a friend, even in death.

Antigone. Well, I was made for fellowship in love,
Not fellowship in hate.

Creon. Then get you down
Thither, and love, if you must love, the dead!
No woman, while I live, shall order me.

Chorus

See where out by the doors Ismene
Weeping drops of sisterly grieving
Comes; and a cloud o'erhanging her
    eyebrows
Mars her dark-flushed cheek, and
    moistens
Her fair face with pitiful tears.
Enter Attendants with ISMENE.

Creon. And you — who like a viper
    unawares
Have crept into my house, and sucked me
    bloodless,
While I unknowingly was fostering you,
Twin furies, to the upsetting of my
    throne—
Come, tell me, will you say you also
    shared
This burying, or protest your innocence?

Ismene. Yes, I have done it — if Antigone
Says so — I join with her to share the
    blame.

Antigone. That justice will not suffer; you
    refused,
And I — I had no partner.

Ismene.   In your trouble
I do not blush to claim companionship
Of what you have to endure.

Antigone.   Whose was the deed
Death and the spirits of the dead can tell!

A friend in words is not a friend for me.
Ismene. Shame me not, sister, by denying
  me
  A death, for honouring the dead, with
    you!
Antigone. Mix not your death with mine.
  Do not claim work
  You did not touch. I shall suffice to die.
Ismene. And what care I for life, if I lost
  you?
Antigone. Ask Creon; you are dutiful to
  him.
Ismene. Why do you cross me so, to no good
  purpose?
Antigone. Nay, I am sick at heart, if I do
  make
  My mock of you.
Ismene.   Nay but what can I do,
  Now, even yet, to help you?
Antigone.   Save yourself;
  I do not grudge you your escape.
Ismene.   O me
  Unhappy! And must I miss to share your
    fate?
Antigone. You made your choice, to live; I
  mine, to die.
Ismene. Not if you count my words unsaid.
Antigone.   By some
  Your judgment is approved; by others
  mine.

31

Ismene. Then our delinquency is equal, too.

Antigone. Take courage, you are living; but
   my life

  Long since has died, so I might serve the
  dead.

Creon. Of these two girls I swear the one
   even now

  Has been proved witless; the other was so
  born.

Ismene. Ah sir, the wretched cannot keep
   the wit

  That they were born with, but it flits
  away.

Creon. Yours did so, when you chose to join
   ill-doers

  In their misdoing.

Ismene. How could I live on
  Alone, without my sister?

Creon. Do not say
  "My sister"; for you have no sister more.

Ismene. What, will you put to death your
   own son's bride?

Creon. He may go further afield—

Ismene. Not as by troth
  Plighted to her by him.

Creon. Unworthy wives
  For sons of mine I hate.

Antigone. O dearest Haemon,
  How are you slighted by your father!

Creon. I

32

Am weary of your marriage, and of you.
Ismene. Your own son! will you tear her
    from his arms?
Creon. Death will prevent that bridal-rite,
    for me.
I Senator. I see, the sentence of this
    maiden's death
Has been determined.
Creon.   Then we see the same.
    An end of trifling. Slaves, there, take
        them in!
    As women, henceforth, must they live —
        not suffered
    To gad abroad; for even bold men flinch,
    When they view Death hard by the verge
        of Life.
    [Exeunt ANTIGONE and ISMENE,
                guarded.
            Chorus.
            I. 1.
Happy the man whose cup of life is free
    From taste of evil! If Heaven's influence
        shake them,
    No ill but follows, till it overtake them,
All generations of his family;
        Like as when before the sweep
            Of the sea-borne Thracian blast
            The surge of ocean coursing past
        Above the cavern of the deep
        Rolls up from the region under

All the blackness of the shore,
And the beaten beaches thunder
Answer to the roar.

I. 2.

Woes upon woes on Labdacus' race I see—
Living or dead — inveterately descend;
And son with sire entangled, without end,
And by some God smitten without remedy;
For a light of late had spread
O'er the last surviving root
In the house of Oedipus;
Now, the sickle murderous
Of the Rulers of the dead,
And wild words beyond control,
And the frenzy of her own soul,
Again mow down the shoot.

II. 1.

Thy power, O God, what pride of man
constraineth,
Which neither sleep, that all things else
enchaineth,
Nor even the tireless moons of Heaven
destroy?
Thy throne is founded fast,
High on Olympus, in great brilliancy,
Far beyond Time's annoy.
Through present and through future and
through past
Abideth one decree;
Nought in excess

Enters the life of man without
  unhappiness.

II. 2.

For wandering Hope to many among
  mankind
Seems pleasurable; but to many a mind
  Proves but a mockery of its wild desires.
  They know not aught, nor fear,
  Till their feet feel the pathway strewn
    with fires.
  "If evil good appear,
  That soul to his ruin is divinely led"—
    (Wisely the word was said!)
    And short the hour
He spends unscathed by the avenging
  power.
    Haemon comes, thy last surviving
    Child. Is he here to bewail, indignant,
    His lost bride, Antigone? Grieves he
      For a vain promise — her
      marriage-bed?
    Enter HAEMON.

Creon. We shall know soon, better than
  seers can tell us.
  Son, you are here in anger, are you not,
  Against your sire, hearing his final doom
  Upon your bride to be? Or are we friends,
  Always, with you, whate'er our policy?
Haemon. Yours am I, father; and you guide
  my steps

With your good counsels, which for my
    part   I
Will follow closely; for there is no
    marriage
Shall occupy a larger place with me
Than your direction, in the path of
    honour.
Creon. So is it right, my son, to be
    disposed—
In everything to back your father's
    quarrel.
It is for this men pray to breed and rear
In their homes dutiful offspring — to
    requite
The foe with evil, and their father's friend
Honour, as did their father. Whoso gets
Children unserviceable — what else could
    he
Be said to breed, but troubles for himself,
And store of laughter for his enemies?
Nay, never fling away your wits, my son,
Through liking for a woman; recollect,
Cold are embracings, where the wife is
    naught,
Who shares your board and bed. And
    what worse sore
Can plague us, than a loved one's
    worthlessness?
Better to spurn this maiden as a foe!

Leave her to wed some bridegroom in the
　　grave!
For, having caught her in the act, alone
Of the whole city disobeying me,
I will not publicly bely myself,
But kill her. Now let her go glorify
Her God of kindred! If I choose to cherish
My own born kinsfolk in rebelliousness,
Then verily I must count on strangers
　　too.
For he alone who is a man of worth
In his own household will appear upright
In the state also; and whoe'er offends
Against the laws by violence, or thinks
To give commands to rulers — I deny
Favour to such. Obedience is due
To the state's officer in small and great,
Just and unjust commandments; he who
　　pays it
I should be confident would govern well,
And cheerfully be governed, and abide
A true and trusty comrade at my back,
Firm in the ranks amid the storm of war.
There lives no greater fiend than
　　Anarchy;
She ruins states, turns houses out of
　　doors,
Breaks up in rout the embattled soldiery;
While Discipline preserves the multitude
Of the ordered host alive. Therefore it is

We must assist the cause of order; this
Forbids concession to a feminine will;
Better be outcast, if we must, of men,
Than have it said a woman worsted us.
I Senator. Unless old age have robbed me of
 myself,
I think the tenor of your words is wise.
Haemon. Father, the Gods plant reason in
 mankind,
Of all good gifts the highest; and to say
You speak not rightly in this, I lack the
 power;
Nor do I crave it. Still, another's thought
Might be of service; and it is for me,
Being your son, to mark the words, the
 deeds,
And the complaints, of all. To a private
 man
Your frown is dreadful, who has things to
 say
That will offend you; but I secretly
Can gather this; how the folk mourn this
 maid,
"Who of all women most unmeriting,
For noblest acts dies by the worst of
 deaths,
Who her own brother battle-slain —
 unburied—
Would not allow to perish in the fangs
Of carrion hounds or any bird of prey;

And" (so the whisper darkling passes
　　round)
"Is she not worthy to be carved in gold?"
Father, beside your welfare there is
　　nothing
More prized by me; for what more
　　glorious crown
Can be to children, than their father's
　　honour?
Or to a father, from his sons, than theirs?
Do not persist, then, to retain at heart
One sole idea, that the thing is right
Which your mouth utters, and nought
　　else beside.
For all men who believe themselves alone
Wise, or that they possess a soul or
　　speech
Such as none other, turn them inside out,
They are found empty; and though a man
　　be wise,
It is no shame for him to live and learn,
And not to stretch a course too far. You
　　see
How all the trees on winter torrent banks,
Yielding, preserve their sprays; those that
　　would stem it
Break, roots and all; the shipman too, who
　　keeps
The vessel's main sheet taut, and will not
　　slacken,

Goes cruising, in the end, keel uppermost:
Let thy wrath go! Be willing to relent!
For if some sense, even from a younger
　head,
Be mine to afford, I say it is far better
A man should be, for every accident,
Furnished with inbred skill; but what of
　that?
Since nature's bent will have it otherwise,
'Tis good to learn of those who counsel
　wisely.

I Senator. Sir, you might learn, when he
　speaks seasonably;
And you, from him; for both have spoken
　well.

Creon. Men that we are, must we be sent to
　school
To learn discretion of a boy like this?

Haemon. None that's dishonest; and if I am
　young,
It is not well to have regard to years
Rather than services.

Creon.　　　　　　　　Good service is it,
To pay respect to rebels?

Haemon.　　　　　　　　To wrongdoers
I would not even ask for reverence.

Creon. Was it not some such taint infected
　her?

Haemon. So say not all this populace of
　Thebes.

Creon. The city to prescribe me my decrees!

Haemon. Look, say you so, you are too
    young in this!

Creon. Am I to rule this land after some will
    Other than mine?

Haemon.   A city is no city
    That is of one man only.

Creon.   Is not the city
    Held to be his who rules it?

Haemon.   That were brave—
    You, a sole monarch of an empty land!

Creon. This fellow, it seems, fights on the
    woman's side.

Haemon. An you be woman! My
    forethought is for you.

Creon. O villain — traversing thy father's
    rights!

Haemon. Because I see you sinning against
    right.

Creon. Sin I, to cause my sway to be held
    sacred?

Haemon. You desecrate, by trampling on
    Heaven's honour.

Creon. Foul spotted heart — a woman's
    follower!

Haemon. You will not find me serving what
    is vile.

Creon. I say this talk of thine is all for her.

Haemon. And you, and me, and for the
    Gods beneath!

Creon. Never shall she live on to marry thee!

Haemon. Die as she may, she shall not die
alone.

Creon. Art thou grown bold enough to
threaten, too?

Haemon. Where is the threat, to speak
against vain counsel?

Creon. Vain boy, thyself shalt rue thy
counselling.

Haemon. I had called you erring, were you
not my sire.

Creon. Thou woman's bondman, do not
spaniel me!

Haemon. Do you expect to speak, and not
be answered?

Creon. Do I so? By Olympus over us,
If thou revile me, and find fault with me,
Never believe but it shall cost thee dear!
Bring out the wretch, that in his sight, at
once,
Here, with her bridegroom by her, she
may die!

Haemon. Not in my sight, at least — not by
my side,
Believe it, shall she perish! And for thee—
Storm at the friends who choose thy
company!
My face thou never shalt behold again.
[Exit.

I Senator. The man is gone, my lord,
　　headlong with rage;
　And wits so young, when galled, are full of
　　danger.

Creon. Let be, let him imagine more, or do,
　Than mortal may; yet he shall not redeem
　From sentence those two maidens.

I Senator. 　　　　　　　　Both of them?
　Is it your will to slay them both alike?

Creon. That is well said; not her who did not
　　touch it.

I Senator. And by what death mean you to
　　kill the other?

Creon. Into some waste untrodden of
　　mankind
　She shall be drawn, and, in some rock-
　　hewn cave,
　With only food enough provided her
　For expiation, so that all the city
　Escape the guilt of blood, buried alive.
　There, if she ask him, Hades, the one God
　Whom she regards, may grant her not to
　　perish;
　Or there, at latest, she shall recognize
　It is lost labour to revere the dead. *[Exit.*

Chorus.

O Love, thou art victor in fight: thou mak'st
　all things afraid;
Thou couchest thee softly at night on the
　cheeks of a maid;

43

Thou passest the bounds of the sea, and the
    folds of the fields;
To thee the immortal, to thee the ephemeral
    yields;
Thou maddenest them that possess thee;
    thou turnest astray
The souls of the just, to oppress them, out of
    the way;
Thou hast kindled amongst us pride, and
    the quarrel of kin;
Thou art lord, by the eyes of a bride, and the
    love-light therein;
Thou sittest assessor with Right; her
    kingdom is thine,
Who sports with invincible might,
    Aphrodita divine.

    Enter ANTIGONE, guarded.
I too, myself, am carried as I look
Beyond the bounds of right;
Nor can I brook
The springing fountain of my tears, to see
My child, Antigone,
Pass to the chamber of universal night.

      I. 1.

Antigone. Behold me, people of my native
    land:
   I wend my latest way:
   I gaze upon the latest light of day
    That I shall ever see;
   Death, who lays all to rest, is leading me

To Acheron's far strand
Alive; to me no bridal hymns belong,
  For me no marriage song
Has yet been sung; but Acheron instead
  Is it, whom I must wed.
Chorus. Nay but with praise and voicings of
    renown
Thou partest for that prison-house of the
  dead;
Unsmitten by diseases that consume,
  By sword unvisited,
Thou only of mortals freely shalt go down,
  Alive, to the tomb.

I. 2.

Antigone. I have heard tell the sorrowful
    end of her,
  That Phrygian sojourner
On Sipylus' peak, offspring of Tantalus;
  How stony shoots upgrown
Like ivy bands enclosed her in the stone;
  With snows continuous
And ceaseless rain her body melts away;
  Streams from her tear-flown head
Water her front; likest to hers the bed
  My fate prepares today.
Chorus. She was of godlike nature,
    goddess-sprung,
And we are mortals, and of human race;
  And it were glorious odds
  For maiden slain, among

The equals of the Gods
In life — and then in death — to gain a
place.

II. 1.

Antigone. They mock me. Gods of Thebes!
why scorn you me
Thus, to my face,
Alive, not death-stricken yet?
O city, and you the city's large-dowered
race,
Ye streams from Dirca's source,
Ye woods that shadow Theba's chariot-
course
Listen and see,
Let none of you forget,
How sacrificed, and for what laws
offended,
By no tears friended,
I to the prisoning mound
Of a strange grave am journeying under
ground.
Ah me unhappy! [home is none for me;]
Alike in life or death an exile must I be.
Chorus. Thou to the farthest verge
forth-faring,
O my child, of daring,
Against the lofty threshold of the laws
Didst stumble and fall. The cause
Is some ancestral load, which thou art
bearing.

II. 2.

Antigone. There didst thou touch upon my
     bitterest bale—
  A threefold tale—
    My father's piteous doom,
  Doom of us all, scions of Labdacus.
    Woe for my mother's bed!
  Woe for the ill-starred spouse, from her
    own womb
  Untimely born!
    O what a father's house
  Was that from whence I drew my life
    forlorn!
  To whom, unwed,
    Accursed, lo I come
  To sojourn as a stranger in their home!
  And thou too, ruined, my brother, in a
    wife,
Didst by thy death bring death upon thy
    sister's life!

Chorus. To pay due reverence is a duty, too:
  And power — his power, whose empire is
    confest,
  May no wise be transgressed;
  But thee thine own infatuate mood
    o'er-threw.

Antigone. Friendless, unwept, unwed,
  I, sick at heart, am led
    The way prepared for me;
      Day's hallowed orb on high

I may no longer see;
For me no tears are spent,
Nor any friends lament
   The death I die.
    Enter CREON.

Creon. Think you that any one, if help might
   be
In wailing and lament before he died,
Would ever make an end? Away with her!
Wall her up close in some deep catacomb,
As I have said; leave her alone, apart,
To perish, if she will; or if she live,
To make her tomb her tenement. For us,
We will be guiltless of this maiden's
   blood;
But here on earth she shall abide no more.

Antigone. Thou Grave, my bridal chamber!
   dwelling-place
Hollowed in earth, the everlasting prison
Whither I bend my steps, to join the band
Of kindred, whose more numerous host
   already
Persephone hath counted with the dead;
Of whom I last and far most miserably
Descend, before my term of life is full;
I come, cherishing this hope especially,
To win approval in my father's sight,
Approval too, my mother, in thine, and
   thine

Dear brother! for that with these hands I
    paid
Unto you dead lavement and ordering
And sepulchre-libations; and that now,
Polynices, in the tendance of thy body
I meet with this reward. Yet to the wise
It was no crime, that I did honour thee.
For never had I, even had I been
Mother of children, or if spouse of mine
Lay dead and mouldering, in the state's
    despite
Taken this task upon me. Do you ask
What argument I follow here of law?
One husband dead, another might be
    mine;
Sons by another, did I lose the first;
But, sire and mother buried in the grave,
A brother is a branch that grows no more.
Yet I, preferring by this argument
To honour thee to the end, in Creon's
    sight
Appear in that I did so to offend,
And dare to do things heinous, O my
    brother!
And for this cause he hath bid lay hands
    on me,
And leads me, not as wives or brides are
    led,
Unblest with any marriage, any care
Of children; destitute of friends, forlorn,

Yet living, to the chambers of the dead
See me descend. Yet what celestial right
Did I transgress? How should I any more
Look up to heaven, in my adversity?
Whom should I call to aid? Am I not come
Through piety to be held impious? If
This is approved in Heaven, why let me
  suffer,
And own that I have sinned; but if the sin
Belong to these — O may their punish-
  ment
Be measured by the wrongfulness of
  mine!

I Senator. Still the same storms possess her,
  with the same
Precipitance of spirit.

Creon.   Then for this
Her guards shall rue their slowness.

Antigone.   Woe for me!
The word I hear comes hand in hand with
  death!

I Senator. I may not say Be comforted, for
  this
Shall not be so; I have no words of cheer.

Antigone. O City of Theba! O my country!
  Gods,
The Fathers of my race! I am led hence—
I linger now no more. Behold me, lords,
The last of your kings' house — what
  doom is mine,

And at whose hands, and for what cause
  — that I
Duly performed the dues of piety!
    [Exeunt ANTIGONE and guards.
      Chorus.
       I. 1.

For a dungeon brazen-barred
  The body of Danae endured
    To exchange Heaven's daylight of
    old,
  In a tomb-like chamber immured,
Hid beneath fetter and guard;
And she was born, we are told,
  O child, my child, unto honour,
  And a son was begotten upon her
To Zeus in a shower of gold.
But the stress of a Fate is hard;
Nor wealth, nor warfare, nor ward,
  Nor black ships cleaving the sea
  Can resist her, or flee.
       I. 2.

And the Thracians' king, Dryas' son,
  The hasty of wrath, was bound
    For his words of mocking and pride:
  Dionysus closing him round,
Pent in a prison of stone;
Till, his madness casting aside
  Its flower and fury wild,
  He knew what God he reviled—
Whose power he had defied;

Restraining the Maenad choir,
Quenching the Evian fire,
  Enraging the Muses' throng,
  The lovers of song.
II. 1.
And by the twofold main
  Of rocks Cyanean — there
    Lies the Bosporean strand,
And the lone Thracian plain
  Of Salmydessus, where
    Is Ares' border-land:
Who saw the stab of pain
  Dealt on the Phineid pair
    At that fierce dame's command;
Blinding the orbits of their blasted sight,
Smitten, without spear to smite,
  By a spindle's point made bare,
  And by a bloody hand.
II. 2.
They mourned their mother dead,
  Their hearts with anguish wrung,
    Wasting away, poor seed
Of her deserted bed;
  Who, Boreas' daughter, sprung
    From the old Erechtheid breed,
In remote caverns fed
  Her native gales among,
    Went swiftly as the steed,
Offspring of Heaven, over the steep-dow
  wild;

Yet to her too, my child,
>   The Destinies, that lead
>>   Lives of long ages, clung.
>   *Enter TIRESIAS led by a boy.*

Tiresias. Princes of Thebes, two fellow-
>   travellers.

Debtors in common to the eyes of one,

We stand before you; for a blind man's
>   path

Hangs on the guide who marshals him the
>   way.

Creon. What would'st thou now, reverend
>   Tiresias?

Tiresias. That will I tell. Do thou obey the
>   seer.

Creon. I never have departed hitherto
From thy advice.

Tiresais. And therefore 'tis, thou steerest
The city's course straight forward.

Creon.   Thou hast done me
Good service, I can witness.

Tiresias.   Now again
>   Think, thou dost walk on fortune's
>   razor-edge.

Creon. What is it? I tremble but to see thee
>   speak.

Tiresias. Listen to what my art foreshad-
>   oweth,

And thou shalt know. I lately, taking seat
On my accustomed bench of augury,

Whither all tribes of fowl after their kind
Alway resort, heard a strange noise of
  birds
Screaming with harsh and dissonant
  impetus;
And was aware how each the other tore
With murderous talons; for the whirr of
  wings
Rose manifest. Then feared I, and
  straight made trial
Of sacrifices on the altar-hearths
All blazing; but, out of the offerings,
There sprang no flame; only upon embers
  charred
Thick droppings melted off the
  thigh-pieces,
And heaved and sputtered, and the
  gall-bladders
Burst, and were lost, while from the folds
  of fat
The loosened thigh-bones fell. Such
  auguries,
Failing of presage through the unseem-
  liness
Of holy rites, I gather from this lad,
Who is to me, as I to others, guide.
And this state-sickness comes by thy
  self-will;
For all our hearths and altars are defiled

With prey of dogs and fowl, who have
  devoured
The dead unhappy son of Oedipus.
Therefore the Gods accept not of us now
Solemn peace-offering or burnt sacrifice,
Nor bird trills out a happy-boding note,
Gorged with the fatness of a slain man's
  blood.
This, then, my son, consider; that to err
From the right path is common to
  mankind;
But having erred, that mortal is no more
Losel or fool, who medicines the ill
Wherein he fell, and stands not obstinate.
Conceit of will savours of emptiness.
Give place, then, in the presence of the
  dead.
Wound not the life that's perished.
  Where's thy valour
  In slaying o'er the slain? Well I advise,
Meaning thee well; 'tis pleasantest to
  learn
Of good advisers, when their words bring
  gain.
Creon. Old man, ye all, like archers at a
  mark,
  Are loosing shafts at me; I am not spared
  Even your soothsayers' practice; by
  whose tribe

Long since have I been made as mer-
  chandize,
And bought, and sold. Gather your gains
  at will!
Market your Sardian silver, Indian gold!
That man ye shall not cover with a tomb;
Not though the eagle ministers of Jove
To Jove's own throne should bear their
  prey of him,
Not even for horror at such sacrilege
Will I permit his burial. This I know;
There is no power in any man to touch
The Gods with sacrilege; but foul the falls
Which men right cunning fall, Tiresias—
Old man, I say — when for the sake of
  gain
They speak foul treason with a fair
  outside.

Tiresias. Alas, does no man know, does no
  man think—

Creon. What should one think? What
  common saw is this?

Tiresias. How far good counsel passes all
  things good?

Creon. So far, I think, folly's the worst of
  harm!

Tiresias. That is the infirmity that fills thy
  nature.

Creon. I care not to retort upon thee, seer.

Tiresias. Thou dost, thou say'st my oracles
    are false.

Creon. All the prophetic tribe are covetous.

Tiresias. And that of kings fond of
    disgraceful gain.

Creon. Know'st thou of whom thou
    speak'st? I am thy lord.

Tiresias. Yea, thou hast saved the state; I
    gave it thee.

Creon. Thou art a wise seer, but in love with
    wrong.

Tiresias. Thou wilt impel me to give
    utterance

To my still dormant prescience.

Creon.   Say on;

Only beware thou do not speak for gain.

Tiresias. For gain of thine, methinks, I do
    not speak.

Creon. Thou shalt not trade upon my wits,
    be sure.

Tiresias. And be thou sure of this; thou shalt
    not tell

Many more turns of the sun's chariot-
    wheel,

Ere thou shalt render satisfaction, one

From thy own loins in payment, dead for
    dead,

For that thou hast made Life join hands
    with Death,

And sent a living soul unworthily

57

To dwell within a tomb, and keep'st a
    corpse
Here, from the presence of the Powers
    beneath,
Not for thy rights or any God's above,
But lawlessly in their despite usurped,
Unhallowed, disappointed, uninterred;
Wherefore the late-avenging punishers,
Furies, from Death and Heaven, lay wait
    for thee,
To take thee in the evil of thine own
    hands.
Look to it, whether I be bribed who speak;
For as to that, with no great wear of time,
Men's, women's wails to thine own house
    shall answer.
Also all cities rise in enmity,
To the strown relics of whose citizens
None pays due hallowing, save beasts of
    prey,
Dogs, or some fowl, whose pinions to their
    gates—
Yes, to each hearth — bear taint defiling
    them.
Such bolts, in wrath, since thou dar'st
    anger me,
I loosen at thy bosom, archer-like,
Sure-aimed, whose burning smart thou
    shalt not shun.

Lead me away, boy, to my own home
    again;
And let him vent his spleen on younger
    men,
And learn to keep a tongue more gentle,
    and
A brain more sober, than he carries now.
        [Exeunt TIRESIAS and Boy.

I Senator. The seer is gone, my lord,
    denouncing woe;
And from the day my old hairs began to
    indue
Their white for black, we have known him
    for a watch
Who never barked to warn the state in
    vain.

Creon. I know it too; and I am ill at ease;
'Tis bitter to submit; but Ate's hand
Smites bitterly on the spirit that abides
    her.

I Senator. Creon Menoeceus' son, be wise
    at need!

Creon. What should I do? speak, I will
    hearken.

I Senator.   Go,
  Set free the maiden from the vault, and
    build
  A tomb for that dead outcast.

Creon.   You approve it?
  You deem that I should yield?

I Senator.   Sir, with all speed.
  Swift-footed come calamities from Heaven
  To cut off the perverse.

Creon.   O God, 'tis hard!
  But I quit heart, and yield; I cannot fight
  At odds with destiny.

I Senator.   Up then, to work!
  Commit it not to others!

Creon.   I am gone
  Upon the instant. Quickly, quickly men,
  You and your fellows, get you, axe in hand,
  Up to the place, there, yonder; and because
  I am thus minded, other than before,
  I who did bind her will be there to loose;
  For it misgives me it is best to keep
  The old appointed laws, all our life long.
        Exeunt CREON and Attendants.

Chorus.

I. 1.

Thou by many names addrest,
Child of Zeus loud-thundering,
Glory of a Theban maid,
Who unbidden wanderest
  Fair Italia's King,
And art lord in each deep glade
Whither all men seek to her,
Eleusinian Demeter;

Bacchus, who by soft-flowing waters
Of Ismenus habitest
Theba, mother of Bacchant daughters,
With the savage Dragon's stock,

I. 2.

Thee the lurid wild-fire meets
O'er the double-crested rock,
Where Corycian Nymphs arow
Bacchic-wise ascending go,
   Thee Castalia's rill;
Thee the ivy-covered capes
Usher forth of Nysa's hill,
And the shore with green of grapes
Clustering, where the hymn to thee
Rises up immortally,
Visitant in Theban Streets,
"Evoe, O Evoe!"

II. 1.

Wherefore, seeing thy City thus—
City far above all other
Dear to thee, and her, thy mother
Lightning-slain — by sickness grievous
Holden fast in all her gates,
Come with quickness to relieve us,
By the slopes of Parnasus,
   Or the roaring straits.

II. 2.

Hail to thee, the first advancing
In the stars' fire-breathing chorus!
Leader of the nightly strain,

Boy and son of Zeus and King!
Manifest thyself before us
With thy frenzied Thyiad train,
Who their lord Iacchus dancing
    Praise, and all night sing.
     Enter a MESSENGER.

Messenger. You citizens who dwell beside
    the roof
Of Cadmus and Amphion, there is no sort
Of human life that I could ever praise,
Or could dispraise, as constant; Fortune
    still
Raising and Fortune overthrowing still
The happy and the unhappy; and none can
    read
What is set down for mortals. Creon,
    methought
Was enviable erewhile, when he preserved
This land of Cadmus from its enemies,
And took the country's absolute
    monarchy,
And ruled it, flourishing with a noble
    growth
From his own seed; and now, he has lost
    all.
For when men forfeit all their joys in life,
One in that case I do not count alive,
But deem of him as of some animate
    corse.

Pile now great riches, if thou wilt, at
  home;
Wear thou the living semblance of a king;
An if delight be lacking, all the rest
I would not purchase, as compared with
  joy,
From any, for the shadow of a shade.

I Senator. What new affliction to the royal
  stock
Com'st thou to tell?

Messenger. Death is upon them — death
Caused by the living.

I Senator.   And who is the slayer?
Speak! who the victim?

Messenger.   Haemon is no more;
His life-blood spilt, and by no stranger's
  hand.

I Senator. What, by his father's, or his own?

Messenger.   Self-slaughtered;
Wroth with his father for the maiden
  slain.

I Senator. Prophet! how strictly is thy word
  come true!

Messenger. Look to the future, for these
  things are so.

I Senator. And I behold the poor Eurydice
Come to us from the palace, Creon's wife;
Either of chance, or hearing her son's
  name.

Enter EURYDICE.

Eurydice. O all you citizens, I heard the
    sound
  Of your discourse, as I approached the
    gates,
  Meaning to bring my prayers before the
    face
  Of Pallas; even as I undid the bolts,
  And set the door ajar, a voice of woe
  To my own household pierces through my
    ears;
  And I sink backward on my handmaidens
  Afaint for terror; but whate'er the tale,
  Tell it again; I am no novice, I,
  In misery, that hearken.
Messenger.   Dear my mistress,
  I saw, and I will speak, and will let slip
  No syllable of the truth. Why should we
    soothe
  Your ears with stories, only to appear
  Liars thereafter? Truth is alway right.
  —I followed in attendance on your lord,
  To the flat hill-top, where despitefully
  Was lying yet, harried by dogs, the body
  Of Polynices. Pluto's name, and hers,
  The wayside goddess, we invoked, to stay
  Their anger and be favourable; and him
  We washed with pure lustration, and
    consumed
  On fresh-lopped branches the remains of
    him,

And piled a monument of natal earth
High over all; thence to the maiden's cell,
Chamber of death, with bridal couch of
  stone,
We made as if to enter. But afar
One fellow hears a loud uplifted wail
Fill all the unhallowed precinct; comes,
  and tells
His master, Creon; the uncertain sound
Of piteous crying, as he draws more nigh,
Comes round him, and he utters, groan-
  ing loud
A lamentable plaint; "Me miserable!
Was I a prophet? Is this path I tread
The unhappiest of all ways I ever went?
My son's voice thrills my ear. What ho,
  my guard!
Run quickly thither to the tomb where
  stones
Have been dragged down to make an
  opening,
Go in and look, whether I really hear
The voice of Haemon, or am duped by
  Heaven."
Quickly, at our distracted lord's
  command,
We looked: and in the tomb's inmost
  recess
Found we her, as she had been hanged by
  the neck,

Fast in a strip-like loop of linen; and him
Laid by her, clasping her about the waist,
Mourning his wedlock severed in the
    grave,
And his sire's deeds, and his ill-fated
    bride.
He, when he sees them, with a terrible cry
Goes in toward him, calling out aloud
"Ah miserable, what hast thou done?
    what mind
Hadst thou? by what misfortune art thou
    crazed?
Come out, my son,—suppliant I ask of
    thee!"
But with fierce aspect the youth glared
    at him;
Spat in his face; answered him not a word;
Grasped at the crossed hilts of his sword
    and drew it,
And—for the father started forth in
    flight—
Missed him! then, angered with himself,
    poor fool,
There as he stood he flung himself along
Upon the sword-point firmly planted in
The middle of his breast, and, conscious
    yet,
Clings to the maid, clasped in his failing
    arms,

And gasping, sends forth on the pallid
    cheek
Fast welling drops of blood: So lies he,
    dead,
With his arms round the dead; there, in
    the grave
His bridal rite is full; his misery
Is witness to mankind what worst of woe
The lack of counsel brings a man to know!
            [Exit EURYDICE.

I Senator. What do you make of this? The
    woman's gone
    Back, and without one word, of good or
    bad!
Messenger. I marvel too; and yet I am in
    hope
    She would not choose, hearing her son's
    sad fate,
    In public to begin her keening-cry;
    But rather to her handmaids in the house
    Dictate the mourning for a private pain.
    She is not ignorant of self-control,
    That she should err.
I Senator.   I know not; but on me
    Weigh heavily both silence over-much,
    And loud complaint in vain.
Messenger.   Well, we shall know it,
    If she hide aught within a troubled heart
    Even to suppression of its utterance,

If we approach the house. Yes, you say
    truly,
It does weigh heavy, silence over-much.
                       [Exit.

Chorus.

Lo now, Creon himself draws near us,
Clasping a record
Manifest, if we sin not, saying it,
Of ruin unwrought by the hands of others,
    But fore-caused by his own self-will.
*Enter CREON, attended, with the body of
HAEMON.*

I. 1.

Creon. O sins of a mind
    That is minded to stray!
    Mighty to bind
    And almighty to slay!
Behold us, kin slayers and slain, O ye who
    stand by the way!
    Ah, newness of death!
       O my fruitless design!
    New to life's breath,
       O son that wert mine,
Ah, ah, thou art dead, thou art sped, for a
    fault
    that was mine, not thine!
I Senator. Ah, how thou seem'st to see the
    truth, too late!
Creon. Ah yes, I have learnt, I know my
    wretchedness!

68

II. 1.

Heaviness hath o'ertaken me
　　And mine head the rod;
The roughness hath shaken me
　　Of the paths I trod;
Woe is me! my delight is brought low, cast
　under the feet of a God!
　　Woe for man's labours that are
　　profitless!
　　Re enter the MESSENGER.
Messenger. O master, now thou hast and
　hast in store
　Of sorrows; one thou bearest in thine
　arms,
　And one at home thou seemest to be come
　Merely to witness.
Creon.　　　　And what more of sorrow,
　Or what more sorrowful, is yet behind?
Messenger. Thy wife, the mother — mother
　of the dead—
　Is, by a blow just fallen, haplessly slain.

I. 2.

Creon. O hard to appease thee,
　　Haven of Death,
　How should it please thee
　　To end this breath?
O herald of heavy news, what is this thy
　mouth uttereth?
　　O man, why slayest thou
　　A man that is slain?

Alas, how sayest thou
      Anew and again
That the slaying of a woman is added to
   slaying — a pain to a pain?

Messenger. See for thyself; the palace doors
   unclose.

*The Altar is disclosed, with the dead body
of Eurydice.*

Creon. Woe is me again, for this new
   sorrow I see.

II. 2.

What deed is not done?
      What tale is not told?
Thy body, O son,
      These arms enfold—
Dead — wretch that I am! Dead, too, is the
   face these eyes behold.
      Ah, child, for thy poor mother! ah for
      thee!

Messenger. She with a sharp-edged dagger
   in her heart
Lies at the altar; and her darkened lids
Close on her wailing for the glorious lot
Of Megareus, who died before, and next
For his, and last, upon her summoning
Evil to fall on thee, the child-slayer!

III. 1.

Creon. Alas, I faint for dread!
      Is there none will deal
      A thrust that shall lay me dead

With the two-edged steel?
Ah woe is me!
I am all whelmed in utter misery!

Messenger. It may be so; thou art arraigned of her
Who here lies dead, for the occasion thou
Hast wrought for Destiny on her, and him.

I Senator. In what way did she slay herself and die?

Messenger. Soon as she heard the raising of the wail
For her son's death, she stabbed herself to the heart.

IV. 1.

Creon. Woe is me! to none else can they lay it,
This guilt, but to me!
I, I was the slayer, I say it,
Unhappy, of thee!
O bear me, haste ye, spare not,
To the ends of earth,
More nothing than they who were not
In the hour of birth!

I Senator. Thou counsellest well — if anything be well
To follow, in calamity; the ills
Lying in our path, soonest o'erpast, were best.

III. 2.

Creon. Come, thou most welcome Fate,
    Appear, O come;
    Bring my days' final date,
      Fill up their sum!
   Come quick, I pray;
   Let me not look upon another day!
I Senator. This for to-morrow; we must take
    some thought
  On that which lies before us; for these
    griefs,
  They are their care on whom the care has
    fallen.
Creon. I did but join your prayer for our
    desire.
I Senator. Pray thou for nothing more; there
    is no respite
  To mortals from the ills of destiny.

IV. 2.

Creon. Lead me forth, cast me out, no other
    Than a man undone;
  Who did slay, unwitting, thy mother
    And thee, my son!
  I turn me I know not where
    For my plans ill-sped,
  And a doom that is heavy to bear
    Is come down on my head.

          [Exit CREON, attended.
         Chorus.
Wisdom first for a man's well-being

Maketh, of all things. Heaven's insistence
Nothing allows of man's irreverence;
And great blows great speeches avenging,
   Dealt on a boaster,
Teach men wisdom in age, at last.

                 [Exeunt omnes.